GILL SAUNDERS

Vintage
Travel Posters

A Journey to the Sea in 30 Posters

Thames & Hudson | V&A

Cover artwork based on:
East Coast by LNER,
Poster designed by Tom Purvis, 1925
(see page 30)

First published in the United Kingdom in 2018 by Thames & Hudson
in association with the Victoria and Albert Museum.

Vintage Travel Posters: A Journey to the Sea in 30 Posters
© 2018 Victoria and Albert Museum/Thames & Hudson

Text and V&A photographs © 2018 Victoria and Albert Museum, London
Design and layout © 2018 Thames & Hudson

Designs by Edward McKnight Kauffer on pp. 17, 19 and 21 are © Simon Rendall;
design by Frank Henry Mason on p.25 is © 2018 Estate of Frank Henry Mason
RBA, RI, RSMA; design by Tristram Hillier on p.35 is © The Estate of Tristram
Hillier/ Bridgeman Images; and designs by Roger Broders on pp.47 and 51 are
© ADAGP, Paris and DACS, London 2018.

British Library Cataloguing-in-Publication Data
A catalogue record for this book is available from the British Library

ISBN 978-0-500-48028-1

Printed and bound in China by C & C Offset Printing Co. Ltd

To find out about all our publications, please visit
www.thamesandhudson.com. There you can subscribe to
our e-newsletter, browse or download our current catalogue,
and buy any titles that are in print.

V&A Publishing
Supporting the world's leading
museum of art and design,
the Victoria and Albert
Museum, London

Holidays by the Sea

Sun, sand and sea – these have long been the essential ingredients for a successful holiday, and this formula was reflected in the multitude of posters that promoted seaside holidays and cruises throughout much of the twentieth century.

The idea of taking a seaside holiday goes back to the eighteenth century, when the health benefits of sea air and bathing in seawater were first recognized. At first of limited appeal, the seaside holiday and the excursion to the coast quickly became popular with all social classes – though a certain snobbery about the busier resorts can be found quite early on. The painter John Constable, in Brighton, Sussex, in 1824 for the sake of his wife's failing health, described the beach there as 'Piccadilly or worse by the seaside', thanks to the hordes of visitors from London. By 1900 almost every town in Britain had a railway station and an extensive rail network linked major cities and industrial towns to sites on the coast. This fostered the growth of day trips and longer stays at the seaside, and led in turn to the development and expansion of the resorts themselves.

From the late nineteenth century onwards holiday resorts in Britain and elsewhere worked in partnership with the railway companies and shipping lines, and publicized their appeal by means of colourful posters picturing their attractions. These posters belong to the golden age of seaside holidays, when resorts marketed themselves as places designed to fulfil the optimistic expectations of holidaymakers who may have looked forward all year to a week at the coast or a trip to the Continent. There is a confidence and a sophistication to the best designs, with their inviting sunlit views, fashion-plate bathers, and smartly dressed couples strolling the promenade or setting sail for distant shores, which reflected the aspirations of their audiences.

Each resort or region was promoted as a desirable destination, with an emphasis on its unique qualities and charms. For some, the landscape was the chief draw and thus the focus of the picture – the golden beaches of Cornwall and the east coast of England, the rugged natural beauty of the Scottish islands, the white cliffs of Normandy, or the blue skies and bluer seas of the Mediterranean coast with its palm trees and pines. While selling the beauties of the natural landscape, the posters often show nature tamed and manicured, the sea held at bay by defences that doubled as gardens or promenades, plentifully supplied with benches, shelters and pavilions for enjoying the view.

The climate was another key selling point. Posters promoting the south coast of England promised sunshine and sea breezes, and in a Southern Railway poster, 'Let's Plan a Holiday', the southern coastal counties are highlighted in sunny yellow. The balmy weather enjoyed by Devon and Cornwall was compared to that of Italy or the French Riviera, and the comparison was enhanced by the planting of exotic flora such as palm trees. Meanwhile the east coast

of Britain was advertised as 'the drier side' of the country; there the resort of Skegness, in a long-running advertisement first published in 1908, made a virtue of its 'bracing' fresh air. The health-giving qualities of sea air (then described as 'ozone') and sea bathing were implicit messages of many posters, and by the 1920s sunbathing was encouraged too, as a suntan, once the mark of outdoor labour, became instead a fashionable sign of wealth and leisure. In views of the Mediterranean and North Africa bright colours and strong shadows emphasize the heat of a landscape basking under cloudless skies.

Beaches, and their associated amenities and entertainments, were popular subjects for posters. Those aimed at families showed brightly painted beach huts, alongside donkey rides and Punch and Judy shows for the children. Decorous scenes of people swimming and sailing, walking and sightseeing were designed to appeal to adult holidaymakers, and to stress a resort's respectability. Acknowledging the unpredictable weather, British resorts were also keen to promote the range of facilities they could offer, not only to compete with other seaside towns but also to broaden their year-round appeal. Attractions featured on posters include lidos and winter gardens, as well as promenades, pavilions and piers, with their sideshows and performances. Likewise, posters for ferries and ocean liners alluded to the comforts available on board, as well as advertising the attractions of their destinations.

Posters for towns such as Brighton in Sussex and Ramsgate in Kent made visual reference to their history and featured their elegant Regency terraces, perhaps to combat the reputation for 'seediness' and vulgarity that gradually attached itself to the more popular (and populous) British seaside resorts. History and architecture were likewise key to the perennial appeal of a major tourist city such as Venice, embodied in a view of the sun-dappled waters of its lagoon. Posters advertising the shipping lines for those travelling further afield – to Canada, the USA, Australia or South America – favoured bold, angular Art Deco views of their ships sailing on calm seas against azure skies, underlining the modernity and the glamour of ocean travel. In short, all these posters, with their vivid and evocative pictures, advertised an escape from everyday life. They offered pleasures to suit everyone, and something for every budget, whether it was a day trip to the coast, a week at the seaside, a channel crossing to the Continent, or a cruise to North Africa, the Far East or Australia.

It was in the 1920s and 1930s that the poster developed as a distinct art form, successfully marrying good graphic design with commercial considerations. Early posters had typically been cluttered, with a collage of images and information competing for attention, and were hard to decipher at a distance. Others were straight reproductions of paintings, presented without regard for how well they might register when seen from afar. This changed in the 1920s with the emergence of specialist poster artists and advertising directors who understood the need for clarity, with image and text in balance. In the best designs, the image dominated, with text reduced to a single simple message and the name of the resort or region alongside the branding for a railway company or a shipping line. Though some railway companies – and also Shell-Mex, a retailer of oil and petrol products, which promoted touring by motor car in a series of now-iconic posters – continued to reproduce paintings in poster format, the most successful and effective posters were those that reflected the new conventions of commercial design.

Holidaymakers were an important source of revenue for the railway companies, and seaside posters were usually displayed on railway station platforms. In Britain, the London and North Eastern Railway (LNER), serving the east coast resorts of England and Scotland, led the way in refining poster design and creating a 'look' that distinguished its brand. The company contracted five artists – including Frank Mason, Frank Newbould and Tom Purvis – who worked exclusively for the company for a given period.

Tom Purvis is now perhaps the best known of the artists contracted to LNER. His characteristic style, with bold, simplified blocks of clear colour, had an immediate visual impact and an Art Deco sophistication. His designs won critical approval, too. A commentator in *The Observer*, in March 1929, wrote: 'He understands the value of elimination and of rendering any subject in its simplest forms and bare essentials. His effective flat patterns explain the design in a flash.' Purvis's posters, like those of the other artists working for LNER in the late 1920s and the 1930s, rarely show a named resort. Instead the posters are generic promotions for 'the East Coast', featuring sunbathers, swimmers, and seaside fun and games.

In the early 1930s the Great Western Railway (GWR) also embarked on an ambitious poster campaign and commissioned six posters promoting Devon and Cornwall from the influential American-born artist and designer Edward McKnight Kauffer. Some of these were uncompromisingly Modernist, with stylized compositions in subtle colours and scenes pictured from unconventional vantage points. Even his more straightforward naturalistic designs appeared consciously 'arty' by comparison with the cheerful pictorial posters by other designers of the time, and they did not enjoy the wide approval from critics and industry that had greeted Purvis's designs – though now of course we can better appreciate Kauffer's exceptional skill and originality.

On the Continent, too, railway companies took the lead in promoting travel to the coast and employed specialist designers – such as the prolific Roger Broders, who designed more than a hundred travel posters for the Paris–Lyon–Mediterranean Railway. In France, posters commissioned by the state railways offered sea bathing, excursions and glorious weather, in Normandy and Brittany, in Monaco, and on the French Riviera. Often more painterly in style than many British posters of the time, they nevertheless employed similar pictorial strategies, with the use of heightened colours in seductive images designed to evoke the prospect of leisure and pleasure in an unspoiled paradise.

Tours to the coast were also promoted by Shell-Mex, a company that encouraged the more discerning holidaymakers (defined as the car-owning middle class) to avoid the popular tourist towns in favour of quieter, more exclusive destinations, generally those that were not served by a railway line and were accessible only by car. Their posters, the work of both established and emerging artists, carried echoes of avant-garde styles such as Surrealism to signal taste and refinement. The contrast with the brasher and more obvious pleasures promoted by the railway companies was a deliberate strategy.

The leisure cruise had been established by the major shipping companies in the late nineteenth century, with P&O and the Orient Line among the pioneers. By the 1920s and 1930s, with well-appointed purpose-built stable ships, sea travel was increasingly seen as a glamorous holiday opportunity, and with commercial expansion what had once been an elite form of recreation became accessible to a wider clientele. Posters promoting transoceanic travel focused on the ships, presenting them as dynamic, streamlined and luxurious; the advertising copy emphasized speed, comfort and exotic destinations. Voyages to Australia and the Far East were seasonal (October to February), so it became standard practice to use the ships for shorter trips in the spring and summer months – these included cruises around the Mediterranean and across to North Africa, or north to the Norwegian fjords. Here the focus of the posters shifted from shipboard luxuries to the attractions of the destinations – the sun-baked Mediterranean landscapes, the palm-fringed coasts, or the serene beauty and magical light to be found in 'the land of the midnight sun'.

Times have changed and it is now the beaches of Spain, the Maldives, Thailand and Florida, among others, that attract holidaymakers in search of dependable sunshine and seaside entertainments, while the cruise, once so exclusive, is now a mass-market leisure pursuit. Posters no longer tempt us from our daily grind – now we look to television and Instagram for seductive seaside imagery – but there is a nostalgic pleasure to be found in these beautiful posters from an earlier age, which remind us of the perennial joys of a holiday by the sea.

Let's Plan a Holiday

Poster designed by Patrick Cokayne Keely
Issued by the Southern Railway, Great Britain, 1932
Colour lithograph
E.199–1935
Given by the Editor of *Commercial Art and Industry*

In the early decades of the 20th century the railway companies led
the way in promoting seaside holidays. This poster was issued by
the Southern Railway, which served resorts along the south coast
of Britain from Kent to Cornwall. In this design a hand holding a red
pencil marks lines on a map radiating out from London to points along
the south coast. While the southern coastal counties are coloured
bright yellow, a set square shadows the remainder of the country –
a neat reference to the various slogans employed by the Southern
Railway, such as 'South for Sunshine'. Pat Keely (1901–70) was a
noted poster artist, much admired for his spare, elegant designs.

 Thames & Hudson | V&A

THE **SOUTH COAST** IS THE **SUNNY COAST**

CHEAPLY BY- 'SUMMER' TICKETS QUICKLY BY-

SOUTHERN RAILWAY

SOUTHERN RAILWAY ADVERTISING

Sanders Phillips & Co., Ltd., THE BAYNARD PRESS, Chryssell Road, S.W.9

The South Coast is the Sunny Coast

Poster designed by Andrew Johnson
Issued by the Southern Railway, Great Britain, 1933
Colour lithograph
E.197–1935
Given by the Editor of *Commercial Art and Industry*

Andrew Johnson (1893–1973) was a prolific commercial designer who worked for the London and North Eastern Railway (LNER) as well as the Southern Railway, and produced a number of posters promoting seaside holidays. This poster, showing two smiling swimsuited women on a beach, has the elegance of a fashion plate, with masterly details such as the rendering of sunlight shining through the translucent brim of the pink sun hat. Like many holiday posters of the period, this does not advertise a named resort, but simply emphasizes the pleasures of a holiday at the seaside.

 Thames & Hudson | V&A

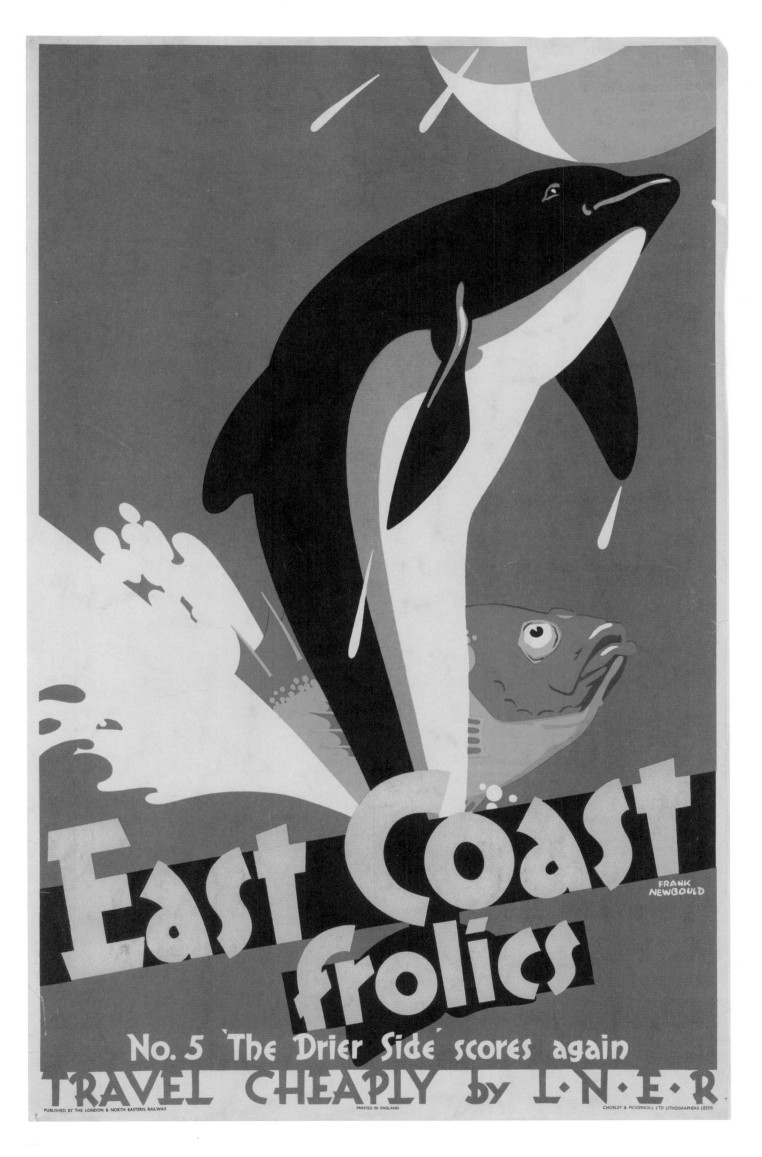

East Coast Frolics.
No.5 'The Drier Side' Scores Again

Poster designed by Frank Newbould
Issued by the London and North Eastern Railway, Great Britain, 1933
Colour lithograph
E.320–1933
Given by the London and North Eastern Railway Co. Ltd

Commissioned by LNER, 'East Coast Frolics' was a series of six humorous designs featuring various creatures – including a frog, fish, rabbit, duck and lobster – enjoying themselves at the seaside. This, the strongest design of the series, shows a dolphin leaping up to head a beach ball. The series was designed to alert potential holidaymakers to the many activities and entertainments available to them in Britain's east coast resorts. In his use of vivacious, almost surreal imagery, the artist seems to be enjoying himself quite as much as his subjects, giving free rein to his inventive wit. With the use of strong primary colours and a jaunty typeface the 'East Coast Frolics' series is typical of the distinctive graphic style of Frank Newbould (1887–1951).

East Coast Frolics.
No.5 'The Drier Side' Scores Again

 Thames & Hudson | V&A

Sutton-on-Sea

Illustrated booklet from Advancement Association, Sutton-on-Sea, or any L·N·E·R Enquiry Office.

Sutton-on-Sea

Poster designed by Tony Castle
Issued by the London and North Eastern Railway, Great Britain, c.1930
Colour lithograph
E.182–1968

Sutton-on-Sea, a small seaside resort in Lincolnshire, on the east coast, was a favourite with families for its sandy beaches. This poster by Tony Castle (1891–1971) emphasizes all the simple pleasures of a family holiday, with rows of homely beach huts along the sands, children busy with their buckets and spades, and their parents relaxing in deckchairs. The deckchair originated in the wood and canvas hammock chair used by the British Army in India, but it was later widely used on the decks of passenger ships, hence the name. Robust and portable, and enforcing a relaxed posture on its occupant, the deckchair became an emblem of seaside leisure.

 Thames & Hudson | V&A

WEYMOUTH

Free Guide from Town Clerk, Weymouth, Dorset.
Express Trains and Holiday Fares by
SOUTHERN RAILWAY

Weymouth

Poster designed by Henry George Gawthorn
Issued by the Southern Railway, Great Britain, c.1931
Colour lithograph
E.1313–1931
Given by the Southern Railway

From the 1780s onwards Weymouth was developed as a seaside resort, thanks to regular visits by King George III and his brother the Duke of Gloucester (who built a residence there); they were attracted by the mild climate and the health benefits of sea bathing. This royal connection, and the elegant Regency terraces along the esplanade, ensured that Weymouth continued to thrive as a fashionable resort, as we can see from this sunlit scene of elegantly dressed bathers. Its designer, Henry George Gawthorn (1879–1941), worked for LNER as well as the Southern Railway.

Saltburn by the Sea

Poster designed by Henry George Gawthorn
Issued by the London and North Eastern Railway, Great Britain, c.1923
Colour lithograph
E.933–1927
Given by the London and North Eastern Railway Co. Ltd

Saltburn by the Sea, North Yorkshire, is famous for its white sands
and for its pier, the only example of its kind in north-east England.
In Gawthorn's vividly coloured view holidaymakers pass through
a ticket office to go down on to the pier, while others stroll along
the esplanade, past the densely planted flower beds, the women
carrying bright parasols for protection from the sun. Gawthorn
often included himself in his poster designs: here, he is the man
in the foreground with binoculars and a panama hat.

 Thames & Hudson | V&A

Go Great Western to Cornwall

Poster designed by Edward McKnight Kauffer
Issued by the Great Western Railway, Great Britain, 1932
Colour lithograph
E.589–1981

Cornwall had developed as a tourist destination owing to the coming
of the railways in the 19th century, and by the 1920s the sandy beaches
and the mild climate had established it as a favourite with British
holidaymakers. It was promoted as a place that was wild, romantic
and remote. The American-born artist Edward McKnight Kauffer
(1890–1954) was commissioned by the Great Western Railway (GWR)
to design six posters to promote Devon and Cornwall. This stylized
view of a path leading between stone walls towards a village, with cliffs
in the background, was one of his more conventional designs, but
his use of simplified forms with strong contrasts of light and shade,
together with his treatment of the lettering, are characteristic
of his Modernist style.

 Thames & Hudson | V&A

GO GREAT WESTERN TO CORNWALL

Go Great Western to Cornwall

Poster designed by Edward McKnight Kauffer
Issued by the Great Western Railway, Great Britain, 1932
Colour lithograph
E.1044-2004
Gift of the American Friends of the V&A; Gift to the American
Friends by Leslie, Judith and Gabri Schreyer and Alice Schreyer Batko

Edward McKnight Kauffer revolutionized poster design in Britain,
introducing a radical Modernist style that often verged on abstraction.
In the early 1930s he was commissioned by GWR to design six posters
promoting Devon and Cornwall. There is a romantic drama to this
design in the Art Deco style, which shows the setting sun, its radiance
silhouetting a bank of cloud as well as the contours of the headlands.
The light gives a metallic sheen and solidity to the arc of waves
swelling into the bay.

 Thames & Hudson | V&A

GO GREAT
TO WESTERN
DEVONSHIRE

PRINTED BY WILLIAM BROWN & CO. LTD., LONDON. E.C.S. & S.E.I.

Go Great Western to Devonshire

Poster designed by Edward McKnight Kauffer
Issued by the Great Western Railway, Great Britain, 1932
Colour lithograph
Circ.402–1971

This is one of six posters that Kauffer designed for GWR to
promote travel to Devon and Cornwall, and it is one of his most
uncompromisingly Modernist designs. Seemingly a view through
sun-dazzled glass across a shimmering blue bay studded with yachts,
it is half-framed in black, as if seen from the window of a train.

 Thames & Hudson | V&A

DUNBAR

FRANK
NEWBOULD

FIRST CLASS GOLF & TENNIS (HARD COURTS)
MODERN HOTELS & BOARDING HOUSES
Full information from Town Clerk, Dunbar, or any L.N.E.R. Enquiry Office

Dunbar

Poster designed by Frank Newbould
Issued by the London and North Eastern Railway, Great Britain, c.1923
Colour lithograph
E.3999–1923
Given by the London and North Eastern Railway Co. Ltd

Dunbar was one of several Scottish resorts served by LNER. Thanks to its location Dunbar gets less rain and more hours of direct sunshine than anywhere else in Scotland, and it is well-connected by rail to Edinburgh and other Scottish towns, so it was soon established as a popular holiday resort. Newbould's inviting bird's-eye view from the top of a steep cliffside pathway looks down on to the lido or outdoor bathing pool. Described at the time as 'the largest swimming pond in Scotland', it reflected contemporary opinion that there was no better or healthier form of exercise than swimming in clean seawater, open to the sun and air. At the time many seaside visitors preferred to swim in the safe confines of a lido, rather than risk the hazards of the sea itself. The Dunbar pool was later demolished as visitor numbers declined.

 Thames & Hudson | V&A

SENTINELS of
BRITAIN'S BEAUTY

FRANK. A. MASON.

ARDNAMURCHAN POINT
AND
ISLANDS OF EIGG AND RUM.

REMEMBER
THE WESTERN HIGHLANDS
NEXT SUMMER

FROM KING'S CROSS

Booklet from L·N·E·R Offices & Agents
READ NOW   VISIT LATER

Sentinels of Britain's Beauty.
Ardnamurchan Point and Islands of Eigg and Rum

Poster designed by Frank Henry Mason
Issued by the London and North Eastern Railway, Great Britain, 1926
Colour lithograph
E.2000-1926
Given by the London and North Eastern Railway Co. Ltd

This is one of a series of six posters issued by LNER, depicting lighthouses around Britain. As well as the Western Highlands of Scotland, shown here, they feature East Anglia, Northumberland and Yorkshire. These posters are unusual for their focus on the dramatic natural beauty of the coastline and the landscapes themselves, rather than on beaches or seaside entertainments. The designer, Frank Henry Mason (1876–1965), was a prolific poster artist, and a painter of seascapes and marine subjects; he had originally trained as a marine engineer before he entered the world of commercial art, and this background is reflected in his sensitive depictions of coastal subjects.

 Thames & Hudson | **V&A**

RAMSGATE

Ramsgate

Poster designed by John Barker
Issued by British Railways, Great Britain, 1954
Colour lithograph
S.5073–1995

John Barker (1911–59), a graphic designer, worked for a time as assistant to the renowned poster artist Austin Cooper. This poster advertising Ramsgate, a seaside resort in Kent, lacks Cooper's economy and clarity but offers instead a charming collage of sights and scenes. Every aspect of the town is set out in neat vignettes – the Regency terraces (many, no doubt, serving as boarding houses), the harbour and the beach, and the promenade illuminated by night, as well as a Punch and Judy show, a child's bucket and spade, and a stall selling shellfish. The nostalgic character of the design is underlined by the 19th-century circus-style lettering of the name Ramsgate printed below.

 Thames & Hudson | V&A

East Coast by LNER

Poster designed by Tom Purvis
Issued by the London and North Eastern Railway, Great Britain, 1925
Colour lithograph
E.744-1925
Given by the London and North Eastern Railway Co. Ltd

Tom Purvis (1888–1959) was one of five leading designers who worked
regularly (and for a time exclusively) for LNER. This design has the
elegant economy of a Japanese woodblock print, and in many ways
it is typical of Purvis's work. By the mid-1920s he had perfected a
sophisticated style in which areas of flat, bright colour were pieced
together like a jigsaw to create images that were legible even when
pasted high on billboards and railway station platforms. This is one
of his most famous poster designs; the sun-drenched colour and the
stylish sunbathers shaded by a parasol bring a flavour of the French
Riviera to the English east coast.

 Thames & Hudson | V&A

BRIDLINGTON

New Guide from Information Bureau or any L·N·E·R Agency

Bridlington

Poster designed by Reginald Edward Higgins
Issued by the London and North Eastern Railway, Great Britain, c.1926
Colour lithograph
E.1017-1926
Given by the London and North Eastern Railway Co. Ltd

The figures in fancy dress walking along the cliffs into the Yorkshire town of Bridlington are pierrots. From the 1890s to the Second World War pierrots were popular British seaside performers. They were inspired by the French pantomime character Pierrot, on whom their distinctive costumes and 'white-face' make-up were based. Pierrot troupes were itinerant entertainers, and performed their song and dance routines on makeshift wooden stages, often set up on the beach itself. Bridlington had been a popular holiday resort since the early 19th century. Reginald Edward Higgins (1877–1933) was a painter and poster artist who worked regularly for LNER.

LOWESTOFT

HIGGINS

WRITE SECRETARY, ADVERTISING COMMITTEE, LOWESTOFT, (ENCLOSING 3ᵈ STAMPS) FOR ILLUSTRATED BOOKLET, ALSO OBTAINABLE FREE ON APPLICATION AT ANY L&N.E.RLY. ENQUIRY OFFICE

Lowestoft

Poster designed by Reginald Edward Higgins
Issued by the London and North Eastern Railway, Great Britain, c.1923
Colour lithograph
E.641–1923
Given by the London and North Eastern Railway Co. Ltd

Higgins's unconventional use of greens, pinks and purples gives a luminous cast to the curls of cloud and the shimmering water. This brings, together with the way in which he has presented the figures in white silhouette, an Art Deco glamour to this view of bathers gathered on the seafront in Lowestoft. Framed like a photograph, the scene is presented as if it were a memento or holiday souvenir. Lowestoft, on the coast of Suffolk, has been a seaside resort since it first became popular as a site for sea-bathing in the 1760s.

 Thames & Hudson | V&A

Tourists Prefer Shell

Poster advertising Shell Motor Spirit, designed by Tristram Hillier
Issued by Shell-Mex and BP Ltd, Great Britain, 1936
Colour lithograph
E.2640–1938
Given by Messrs Shell-Mex Ltd

This Surrealist-flavoured view by Tristram Hillier (1905–83) of a beach below towering white cliffs features a row of gaudy beach huts, but the foreground paraphernalia – a map, pipe, hat and camera – suggests a discerning middle-class traveller, not a day tripper in search of easy entertainment. Unlike the other posters in this Shell series, which are all of named British places, this scene is anonymous, and may be of northern France. Hillier was one of a number of avant-garde artists commissioned by Shell to design posters promoting its motor oil. The campaign was aimed largely at middle-class professionals – doctors, architects, scientists and airmen – as well as tourists, who were encouraged to visit out-of-the-way places, in preference to the sites of mass tourism served by the railways.

 Thames & Hudson | V&A

Goodbye England!   La Belle France!

Short Sea Routes to the Continent by
SOUTHERN RAILWAY
GUIDE BOOKS & TIME-TABLES FROM CHIEF S.R. STATIONS

SOUTHERN RAILWAY ADVERTISING   AD. 1417 1932   Sanders Phillips & Co., Ltd., THE BAYNARD PRESS, Chryssell Road, S.W.9

Goodbye England! La Belle France!

Poster designed by Andrew Johnson
Issued by the Southern Railway, Great Britain, 1930
Colour lithograph
E.358–1931
Given by the Southern Railway Ltd

In this poster, promoting ferry routes to the Continent operated by
the Southern Railway, an exquisitely dressed couple wave farewell
to England and greet their arrival in France with open arms. Andrew
Johnson's stylish design has the sophistication of a fashion plate
and is clearly aimed at well-to-do travellers rather than day trippers.
The Southern Railway claimed that it offered the shortest routes
and fastest journey times for ferry crossings to France from Dover
and Folkestone, and boasted that it 'had transformed the erstwhile
tediousness of travel into a veritable pleasure'. Despite his striking
designs produced in the course of a prolific career as a commercial
artist in the 1920s and 1930s little is known about Andrew Johnson.

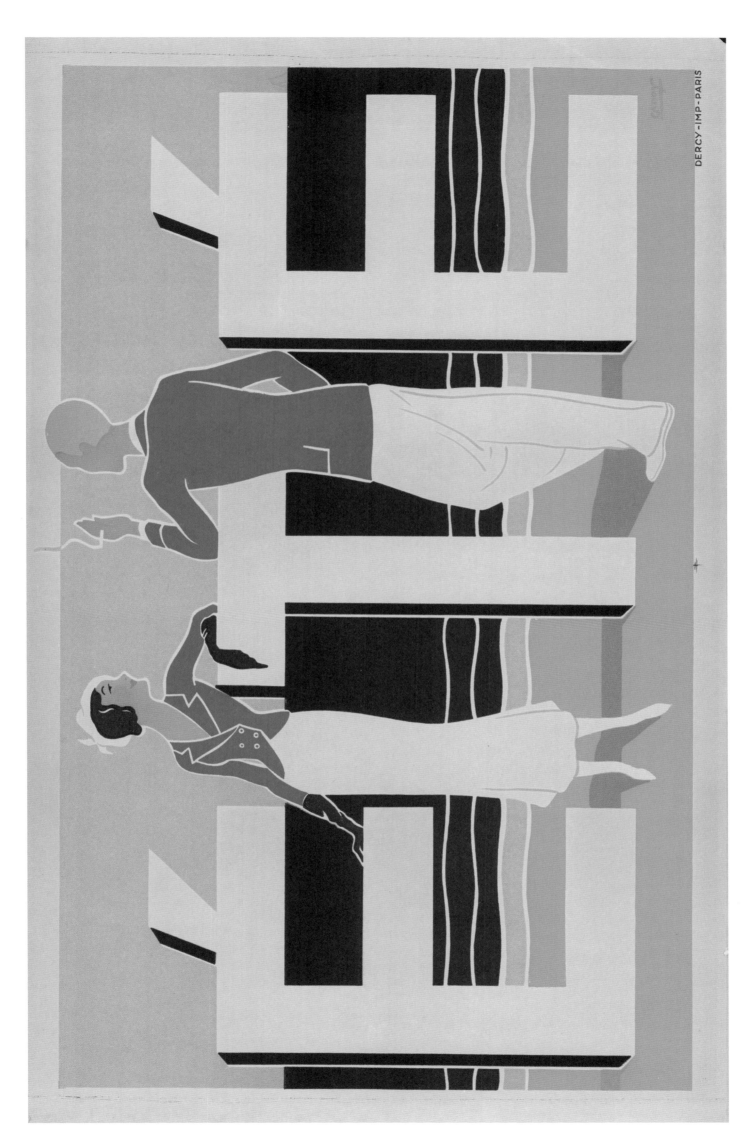

DERCY - IMP - PARIS

Été

Poster designed by Caddy to promote French tourism
France, 1925
Colour lithograph
E.245–1981

Summer in the south of France is conjured up with witty economy
here, with a languidly elegant couple leaning against a seafront
'balustrade' created from the letters of the word *Été* ('summer' in
French). Fashionably dressed and obviously well-to-do, the couple
represent the more sophisticated pleasures of the seaside, those
associated with the resorts of the French Riviera. Despite the
distinctive and confident style of this poster, and the name
'Caddy', the designer is otherwise unknown.

 Thames & Hudson | V&A

CHEMINS DE FER DE L'ÉTAT
LA NORMANDIE EN ÉTÉ
BAINS DE MER ET EXCURSIONS

CORNILLE & SERRE - IMPRIMEURS, 19, Rue du Terrage, PARIS.

La Normandie en Été

Poster designed by Georges Dorival
Issued by Chemins de Fer de l'État (French State Railways), France, c.1914
Colour lithograph
E.175-1922
Given by the Underground Electric Railways Company of London Ltd

In this poster Georges Dorival (1879–1968) has pictured the famous cliffs at Étretat in Normandy, including one of the three natural arches. This striking geology and the nearby beach had previously attracted several notable French artists including Eugène Boudin, Gustave Courbet and Claude Monet. Dorival's view, taken from a vantage point at the top of the cliffs, shows the scene in high summer with a breeze sweeping through the poppies, cornflowers and marguerites flowering among the golden corn stalks, and with ripe blackberries clustered on the gracefully arching bramble branches above. The artist signed the original painting and dated it 1914, but it may have been issued as a poster later.

Thames & Hudson | V&A

CHEMIN DE FER D'ORLÉANS

· COTE · SUD · DE · BRETAGNE ·
· AUDIERNE ·

Cote Sud de Bretagne. Audierne

Poster designed by ALO (Charles-Jean Hallo)
Issued by the Chemin de Fer d'Orléans (Orléans Railway), France, c.1921
Colour lithograph
E.2464–1921
Given by the Underground Electric Railways Company of London Ltd

Charles-Jean Hallo (1884–1969), known as ALO, designed more than a hundred posters for the French railways, many promoting seaside resorts. This view shows Audierne, a modest fishing village on the coast of Brittany. It had been a tourist destination since the railway line opened in 1865, thanks to its wide sandy beaches and picturesque harbour, but the whole region was promoted more vigorously in the 1920s. The appeal of the place is captured in Hallo's poster, with the sails of the fishing boats glowing like Chinese lanterns as they return to the harbour at dusk.

 Thames & Hudson | **V&A**

PARIS-LYON-MÉDITERRANÉE

Julien Lacaze

· LA CÔTE D'AZUR ·
& LE CAP MARTIN ·

FÉDÉRATION DES SYNDICATS D'INITIATIVE DE LA CÔTE D'AZUR & DE LA CORSE, 32 RUE DE L'HÔTEL DES POSTES, NICE

La Côte d'Azur & Le Cap Martin

Poster designed by Julien Lacaze
Issued by the Paris–Lyon–Mediterranean Railway, France, c.1920
Colour lithograph
E.2335–1921
Given by the Paris–Lyon–Mediterranean Railway Company

Cap Martin, on the Côte d'Azur on the Mediterranean coast of France, is noted for its sheltered climate, which has encouraged a rich tropical flora. The Côte d'Azur – also known as the French Riviera – has been popular with visitors (particularly the English aristocracy and later the Americans) for its balmy climate and beautiful landscapes since the late 18th century. Julien Lacaze (1886–1971) produced many travel posters for the Paris–Lyon–Mediterranean (PLM) Railway in the 1920s and 1930s.

 Thames & Hudson | V&A

PARIS - LYON - MÉDITERRANÉE
MONACO
MONTE-CARLO
AU PAYS DU SOLEIL
ROGER BRODERS

Monaco Monte-Carlo au Pays du Soleil

Poster designed by Roger Broders
Issued by the Paris–Lyon–Mediterranean Railway, France, 1921
Colour lithograph
E.2327-1921
Given by the Paris–Lyon–Mediterranean Railway Company

Monte-Carlo, the capital of the principality of Monaco on the French Riviera, has long been a fashionable resort for the wealthy and well-connected, including royalty and film stars. Situated on a prominent escarpment between mountains and sea, it enjoys an idyllic climate, with plentiful sunshine, and is famous for its gardens. All these charms are summed up in this sunlit view by Roger Broders (1883–1953), looking down over the town to the sea from the vantage point of a flower-garlanded pergola on the terrace of a villa or hotel. Broders's later posters were strongly influenced by the Art Deco style, but this is one of his earliest designs, characterized by a more romantic mode.

 Thames & Hudson | V&A

Venice and the Lido

Poster designed by Vittorio Grassi
Issued by Italian State Railways and the State Tourism Department,
London Travel and Tourist Office, Italy, c.1920
Colour lithograph
E.2323–1924
Given by C.G. Holme

Vittorio Grassi (1878–1958) designed a number of posters – based
on his own paintings – for the Italian National Tourist Board in the
1920s and 1930s. In this scene showing the shimmering waters of the
Venetian lagoon, Grassi captured the unique character of the city, with
its luminous sky and distinctive features such as the brightly painted
poles used for mooring gondolas that dominate the foreground. The
poster was produced in two versions – one in Italian and the other in
English – to attract tourists from home and abroad.

 Thames & Hudson | V&A

Marseille. Porte de l'Afrique du Nord

Poster designed by Roger Broders
Issued by the Paris–Lyon–Mediterranean Railway, France, c.1932
Colour lithograph
E.3642-1932
Given by the Underground Electric Railways Company of London Ltd

Marseille had long been a major port, and, as the poster asserts, it was also the gateway from Europe to North Africa, with ferries plying regular routes across the Mediterranean. In this Art Deco-style poster, Broders crafted an almost abstract pattern from the funnels and prows of the ships crowding the harbour, their simple geometry in black, red and white echoing the boldly blocked text below. The design vividly evokes the glamour of foreign travel, before the age of mass tourism. Roger Broders, a French artist and illustrator, is best known for his travel posters promoting tourism in France. Most of his designs were commissioned by the PLM Railway company and it sponsored his travel, allowing him to visit the places he was required to illustrate.

 Thames & Hudson | V&A

HOLIDAY CRUISES TO THE
MEDITERRANEAN
by R·M·S·P
"ARCADIAN"

Holiday Cruises to the Mediterranean
by R M S P 'Arcadian'

Poster designed by Frank Newbould
Issued by the Royal Mail Steam Packet Company, Great Britain, c.1923
Colour lithograph
E.132–1924
Presented by Messrs Sanders Phillips & Co. Ltd

The cruise ship *Arcadian* was created from the salvaged wreck of the *Asturias*, which had been badly damaged by a German torpedo in 1917. After an extensive refit in Belfast, the *Arcadian* cruised the Mediterranean and the West Indies from 1923 to 1930. Frank Newbould's poster was designed to entice tourists with a sun-baked Mediterranean landscape; the location is not specified but is probably North Africa, perhaps Tunis. Newbould was a prolific designer who specialized in travel posters. His clients included London Transport and its predecessors, as well as the Orient and Cunard shipping lines, and the various British railway companies, including LNER. His designs are characterized by flat areas of bright colour and 'cut-out' silhouettes.

 Thames & Hudson | V&A

EMPRESS OF BRITAIN

42,500 TONS · FIVE DAYS CROSSING

CANADIAN PACIFIC

WORLD'S GREATEST TRAVEL SYSTEM

Empress of Britain

Poster designed by J.R. Tooby
Issued by Canadian Pacific Railways, Great Britain, c.1931
Colour lithograph
E.2215–1931
Given by Canadian Pacific Railway Co.

The *Empress of Britain* (built in Scotland between 1928 and 1931) was the second of three Canadian Pacific vessels with the same name. This one provided scheduled passenger services between Canada and Europe from 1931 to 1939. At the time she was the largest and fastest ship on this route. Canadian Pacific attracted customers from the USA and Canada, persuading them to take a train and to sail from Quebec City rather than New York. This route gave passengers an extra day and a half of smooth sailing along the shorter sheltered transatlantic route via the St Lawrence River – and was advertised as '39 per cent less ocean'. In winter, when the river was frozen and crossings suspended, the ship was converted to serve as a luxury cruise liner carrying 700 first-class passengers only. This poster, which exaggerates the streamlined silhouette of the ship seen from below the prow, emphasizes modernity and speed.

 Thames & Hudson | V&A

V. STEIN
MEDITERRANEAN
EGYPT / CEYLON
STRAITS SETTLEMENTS
DUTCH EAST INDIES
AUSTRALIA / CHINA & JAPAN
VIA JAVA
ROTTERDAM LLOYD
ROYAL MAIL LINE

Rotterdam Lloyd Royal Mail Line

Poster designed by Johan Anton Willebrord von Stein
Issued by Rotterdam Lloyd, The Netherlands, 1931
Colour lithograph
E.2567–1931
Given by the Agents of Rotterdam Lloyd Royal Mail Line

Rotterdam Lloyd, a Dutch shipping company, launched the *Baloeran* in 1930, offering a passenger service to the Mediterranean, Egypt, Ceylon (Sri Lanka), Australia, China and Japan. This poster by J.A.W. von Stein (1896–1965) shows the ship sailing into harbour, its bulk and its reflection in the water a dazzling white against the blue of sea and sky. The exotic destinations listed on the poster are hinted at by the stylized palm trees in bold black silhouette in the foreground. The same image was reissued in 1932 to advertise routes to Sumatra and Java.

Thames & Hudson | V&A

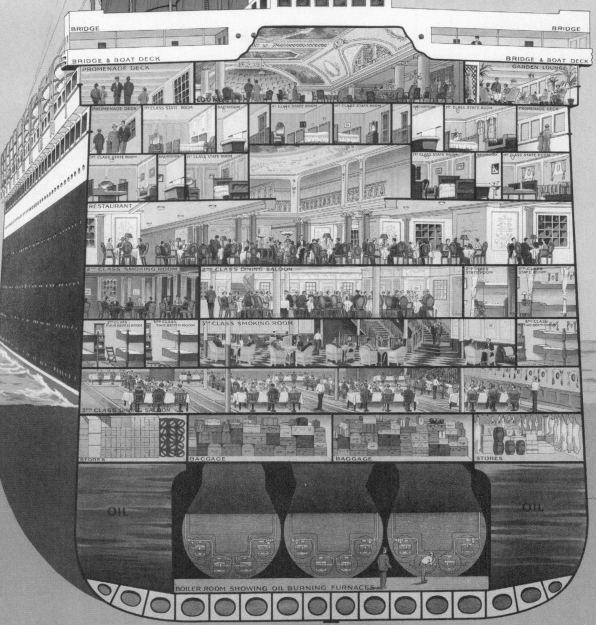

CUNARD LINE

TO ALL PARTS OF THE WORLD

Ulrich Gutersohn   THOS. FORMAN & SONS, NOTTINGHAM, ENGLAND.

Cunard Line. To All Parts of the World

Poster issued by Cunard Line
Great Britain, *c*.1914
Chromolithograph
E.1829-2004
Gift of the American Friends of the V&A; Gift to the American
Friends by Leslie, Judith and Gabri Schreyer and Alice Schreyer Batko

The ship shown here is the *Aquitania*, launched in 1913 to compete
with the more luxurious vessels of the White Star Line. She made her
maiden voyage to New York in 1914. This poster, with its novel cutaway
diagram, reveals the ship's lavish interiors, with promenades and
lounges, and an elegant restaurant decorated in the style of Louis XIV.
Even the third-class accommodation appears spacious, if spartan by
comparison with the first-class facilities above. In a nice detail, we
see the well-stocked stores of food and drink down below. The ship's
interiors were designed by Arthur Joseph Davis, whose firm had also
overseen the construction and decoration of the Ritz Hotel in London.

 Thames & Hudson | V&A

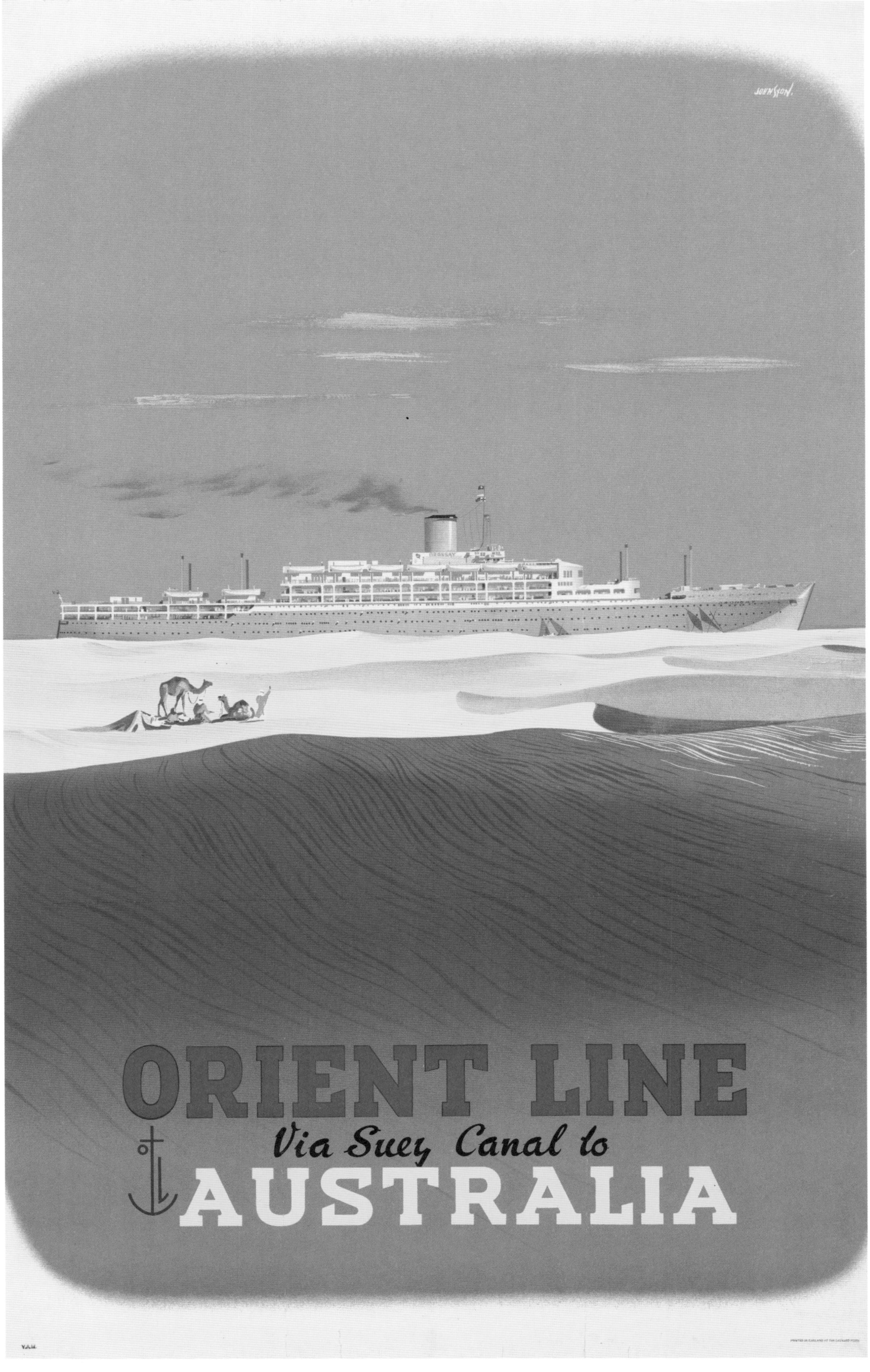
JOHNSTON.
ORIENT LINE
Via Suez Canal to
AUSTRALIA

Orient Line via Suez Canal to Australia

Poster designed by Tom Johnston
Issued by the Orient Steam Navigation Co. Ltd, Great Britain, c.1951
Colour lithograph
E.1892–1952
Given by the Editor of *Modern Publicity*

This ship, the SS *Oronsay*, was completed in 1951 and carried
passengers to Australia via the Suez Canal; it is shown here passing
through the canal in sight of a group of Bedouin with their camels.
The *Oronsay* was the second Orient Line ship to be built after the
Second World War and was noted for her luxurious contemporary
interiors, designed by Brian O'Rourke. In a later claim to fame, the
ship was used for the 'at sea' shots in the British comedy film
Carry on Cruising (1962).

 Thames & Hudson | V&A

ORIENT
LINE
CRUISES NORWAY
13 DAYS from 20 GUINEAS.
APPLY :- 5 FENCHURCH AVENUE   LONDON E.C. 3

Norway

Poster designed by M.V. Jones
Issued by Orient Line Cruises, Great Britain, c.1923
Colour lithograph
E.638–1923
Given by the Underground Electric Railways Company of London Ltd

The Orient Line was originally focused on carrying passengers
and mail to Australia. It continued to do so into the 1950s but the
Australian trade was seasonal, concentrated in the months October
to February. In order to make use of its ships in spring and summer
the Orient Line began offering pleasure cruises to Norway, from the
1880s. Such cruises have remained popular ever since. M.V. Jones, the
designer of this poster, is otherwise unknown but has nevertheless
demonstrated considerable skill in capturing the colour and
atmosphere of the country. The scene of yachts sailing serenely
across a Norwegian fjord has been vividly described, with the
midnight sun giving a vibrant glow to the brilliantly coloured sails.

 Thames & Hudson | V&A